Releasing
OUR CHILDREN TO
GOD

TRUSTING IN HIS PLAN
BEYOND OUR CONTROL

JUANITA TAYLOR

Releasing Our Children to God: Trusting in His Plan Beyond Our Control

Copyright © 2025 by Juanita Taylor

Published by
JT Restoration House Publishing
United States of America

ISBN (Paperback): 979-8-218-91142-3

Cover Design: Temitope Daniel Interior Formatting: Gladys

CONTENTS

ACKNOWLEDGEMENT

Writing this book has been a transformative journey, one marked by faith, surrender, and profound reflection. I could not have taken each step without the grace of God and the unwavering support of the people He has placed in my life.

First, to my mother, Fannie Marlene Aiken, thank you for being the living example of a life anchored in God. Your steadfast faith, consistent prayers, and quiet strength have been a beacon through every season of my life. You taught me how to trust God not just in word but in action, and your legacy of devotion is woven into every page of this book. I am forever grateful for the love you poured into us, the wisdom you have live out daily, and the unwavering foundation of faith and strength you laid. What you instilled in us has shaped who I am today, and for that, I am eternally thankful.

To my beloved husband and children, your patience, love, and encouragement have been my sanctuary. You held me up when I was weary, believed in me when I questioned myself, and reminded me of the beauty of faith in action. Thank you for allowing me the space to pour my heart into this work. You are my inspiration and my why.

To my bonus children, I am grateful for the opportunity to know and love each of you. While I wasn't part of all your journeys from the beginning, it has been a joy and privilege to walk alongside some of you through the seasons of childhood into adulthood.

To Dina, one of my bonus daughters, I've always cherished our transparent talks, your honesty, your strength, and the courage with which you share your heart. Watching you grow into the woman you are today has been a true blessing. Your resilience and thoughtfulness reflect a quiet power that leaves a lasting impact.

To my sister, Auanita, who has always been my personal coach and held me accountable in completing this book. Your encouragement is a gift I treasure deeply. Thank you for pushing me forward when I felt stuck and reminding me why this book matters.

To my family and friends, your prayers, listening ears, and gentle nudges reminded me that I wasn't walking this road alone. Your presence in my life has been a gift, and your encouragement gave me the strength to keep writing when the words felt too heavy to carry.

To Marci, who provided me with valuable feedback and thoughtful insight.

To the two extraordinary women who boldly shared their personal journeys in this book, thank you. Your courage, transparency, and faith will light the way for countless others. You are living proof that God redeems, restores, and writes powerful testimonies through yielded hearts.

And to every parent holding this book in their hands, whether you have biological children or not, this is for you. You may be a godparent, foster parent, spiritual parent, or mentor. I see your heart. I understand your tears. I know what it is to love deeply and still have to release.

May these pages speak life into your weary places, restore your hope, and remind you that you are never alone. Releasing your children into God's hands is not giving up; it is giving them over to the One who created them, knows them intimately, and loves them perfectly.

May this book walk beside you like a trusted friend, offering hope, peace, and a renewed trust in our faithful God.

With deep love and gratitude, Juanita Taylor

PREFACE

In a world where parents silently shoulder the weight of expectations, fears, and an aching desire to shape their children's futures, I found myself torn, caught between unconditional love and the fear of losing control. Releasing control never felt easy or intuitive, but was instead a journey—one marked by heartbreak, surrender, and the transformative pursuit of faith.

This book was born out of those depths, shaped by the vulnerable and soul-stretching process of learning to release my children to God. Not by giving up, but by pressing forward with learning how to trust God. It is the story of walking with God through restless nights and tear- streaked prayers, of gradually learning to loosen my grip on outcomes I could never control, and of discovering peace in His presence, even when the path felt uncertain.

There were moments when their choices shattered my hopes, diverging from the values and truths I had worked so hard to plant.

And yet, in the midst of that pain, I discovered a deeper peace that is unexplainable. Not in the certainty of their path, but in the unwavering presence of God walking beside me. And beside them.

Through these pages, I share the personal lessons God taught me along the way about patience, surrender, prayer, and the quiet strength of release.

I pray that within these words you find pieces of your own journey. That you feel seen, understood, and encouraged. And that you come to know what I now believe with my whole heart: God's timing is always perfect, even when it doesn't make sense to us.

This is not just a story about release. It is a testimony of persistent hope, relentless love, and the miraculous peace that comes when we dare to expect God's faithfulness in life's greatest uncertainties.

Stormie Omartian wrote, "Only when I have released my children completely into God's hands and put the Lord in charge of their lives can I ever have true peace."

That truth deeply moved me. It became more than just a quote; it became a lifeline. Her words stirred something within me and led me to a simple yet life-altering prayer:

"Lord, help me release my children into Your hands. Help me embrace and guide the children You gave me, not the version I imagined they'd be."

That prayer changed everything for me. Releasing, as I came to learn, was not passive. It required courage and daily surrender. It became a conscious decision to trade control for trust, fear for faith, and expectations for grace. It is the invitation to love the children God entrusted to me, while believing that He is writing their stories in ways I may not yet see.

With tenderness and truth, Juanita Taylor

THE BIRTH OF RELEASE

■ ■ ■ ■ ─────────────────────────────

The idea for this version of RELEASE was not born from ease, but from desperation—a soul-deep cry to understand how to parent without breaking, how to trust God while watching my children struggle, and how to hold on to hope when everything in me wanted to control the outcome.

I remember one night, sitting in silence after a difficult conversation with one of my children. My heart was heavy with fear, frustration, and confusion. I had prayed, fasted, and spoken every word I thought might lead them back to the path I believed was right. Yet I was met with silence and uncertainty. In that quiet, I whispered an honest prayer:

"God, how do I release them without giving up? How do I trust You when my heart is breaking?"

The answer didn't come as a lightning bolt, but as a slow, Spirit-led unfolding. God began to show me that releasing my children was not a one-time event—it was a continual posture of the heart. It wasn't about walking away. It was about walking with Him, trusting Him to take the lead.

It taught me to keep learning how to trust, to love without conditions, even when my emotions felt fragile, and to believe that God's plans for my children were far greater than my own. But before I could truly walk this path of release, I had to confront parts of my own story. Buried wounds from my past shaped the way I held on. Letting go felt unsafe because I was still carrying pain I hadn't yet named.

It wasn't until I began to uncover those hidden places—the quiet fears, the disappointments I had buried, and the sorrow I had never fully acknowledged—that I began to loosen my grip and surrender the outcome.

Letting go of control and waiting for God to move in my children's lives was never easy. Releasing them to Him has been one of the hardest things I've ever done, especially when I witnessed them making poor choices or surrounding themselves with harmful influences. My heart longed to intervene, and the pain of watching them struggle often overwhelmed me. And yet, when I placed them fully in God's hands, His peace became my anchor.

This journey of release wasn't passive. It required active faith, inner strength, and continuous surrender. If you've ever wrestled with the tension between love, worry, and letting go, you are not alone.

As parents, we often carry the weight of expectations and fears, with a deep desire to shape our children's futures. This book is born from my personal journey of learning to release my children to God—not with resignation, but with active, steadfast faith. It's about learning to love unconditionally while releasing control over what we can't manage.

Through personal stories, biblical truths, and the experiences of other mothers who have walked similar paths, I hope this book offers guidance and encouragement. Together, we'll explore the scars we carry, the "light bulb" moments that lead to healing, and the transforming power of trusting God.

Over time, the word RELEASE became more than just a word. It evolved into a spiritual framework—shaping my parenting, my prayers, and my posture before God. It became a roadmap, marking my journey through repentance, trust, love, faith, prayer, surrender, and growth.

These weren't abstract principles. They were truths forged in the trenches of motherhood—through tears, tough love, and relentless hope. I didn't discover RELEASE through theory; I lived it. Each letter became a truth I had to learn the hard way—through humility, surrender, and divine grace.

Maya Angelou once said, "Do the best you can until you know better. Then when you know better, do better." That quote became a turning point for me. With a new revelation of God's grace, I was able to parent with greater purpose and compassion.

As you continue reading, I pray that what's shared in these pages will help you recognize your own turning points, release the need for control, and step boldly into the freedom of trusting God with your children.

My healing began with honest reflection, prayer, and a willingness to face myself with humility. Therapy also played a key role—my counselor's questions uncovered emotional patterns I hadn't realized were influencing how I parented. As healing came, I saw that this wasn't just about me—it was about the legacy I'm building for my children, grandchildren, and future generations.

In that sacred space, I found the strength to trust God—not just with words, but with posture. I didn't just let go. I began to lay down my expectations, my fears, and my need to control. And I invited God to lead.

So, I invite you to walk this road with me, one step at a time. May these words meet you with compassion, courage, and clarity. May you come to know that RELEASE is not about letting go in defeat—but about surrendering in trust.

RELEASE became the path that led me from fear-based parenting to faith-filled surrender. These are the seven truths that shaped that journey:

R – Repent: I had to acknowledge and turn from moments where I relied on my own understanding, especially when fear drove my decisions. True healing began when I repented for trying to control what only God could handle.

E – Entrust: I learned to place my children in the hands of the One who created them, even when I didn't understand His timing.

L – Love Unconditionally: I had to love my children without conditions, even when they didn't meet my expectations.

E – Exercise Faith: I chose to believe that God was working behind the scenes, even when I saw no visible change.

A – Abide in Prayer: Prayer became my anchor—connecting my heart to God's peace and perspective.

S – Surrender Control: I stopped trying to fix everything and let God be God.

E – Evolve as a Parent: As my children grew, I had to grow too— shifting from a fixer to a faithful intercessor.

My prayer is that these truths speak life to your journey as they have to mine. May they help you loosen your grip, open your heart, and embrace the beauty of parenting with faith instead of fear.

With love and hope, Juanita

—— Chapter 1 ——

THE HIDDEN SCARS WE CARRY

In this book, I use the word *"residue"* to describe the unseen, lingering effects of unresolved emotional wounds, ingrained beliefs, or behavioral patterns carried into adulthood. These remnants—whether rooted in trauma, learned habits, or negative thought processes—silently shape how we navigate life. They influence how we respond to challenges, regulate emotions, and connect with others, often operating beneath our awareness. While these hidden scars can remain buried for years, they quietly dictate our choices, relationships, and sense of self.

For most of my life, I did not recognize this residue. I had two major traumatic experiences during childhood that left me voiceless. I kept those memories hidden for years, confiding in my husband only much later in our marriage. Unaware of how deeply the pain had influenced me, I masked my emotions behind a composed exterior. On the surface, I appeared strong, competent, and resilient. But beneath the surface, unacknowledged wounds festered. Each accomplishment became a mask, hiding the vulnerable parts of me longing for freedom and healing. No level of success could fill the void left by those unhealed places.

Looking back on my childhood, I remember many moments when I felt inadequate, even though I couldn't always identify why. I sought validation through activities—dance, basketball, violin, clarinet, and track—hoping to find a place where I truly belonged. One moment stands out. During track practice, I fell while trying to jump a hurdle, scraping my knee. I sat alone, blood dripping down my leg, waiting for someone to notice. No one did. Instead of seeking comfort or voicing my pain, I quietly quit and never went back. It wasn't the fall that hurt most—it was the silence that followed.

In large families, a child can easily feel invisible, lost in the crowd. But even in the stillness of smaller households, a child's emotional needs can go unnoticed, unheard, and unmet. For me, growing up with six siblings and a mother who raised us alone after the divorce, our home revolved around survival. Each of us lived in our own bubble, doing what we could to get by. In the constant busyness, no one noticed when I quietly withdrew from school activities. That lack of acknowledgment taught me to suppress my emotions and carry my struggles in silence.

Throughout my grade school years, I often felt emotionally distant from my mother. While I never doubted her love, it wasn't always expressed in a way that encouraged emotional openness. I felt unseen and overlooked, which deepened my sense of inadequacy. Over time, I internalized the belief that my voice didn't matter. Even now, I sometimes hesitate before telling my truth, unsure if it will be accepted or rejected.

At the same time, I saw my mother's unwavering strength. Though she didn't work outside the home, she managed the household, stretched every resource, and made daily sacrifices to keep us going. As a child, I didn't fully understand her resilience, but later I recognized how her deep faith in God had carried us. It may have been all she had, but it was enough.

The emotional baggage I carried long before becoming a parent remained untouched, and childhood wounds quietly influenced my life. I learned to survive by adopting roles that made me feel safe, striving for perfection, chasing achievement, and seeking approval. These roles became masks that offered a fragile sense of control while concealing my inner pain.

They showed up in many ways: obsessing over appearances, performing well, blending into church life, and avoiding emotional vulnerability. In truth, I was trying to escape loneliness and unresolved hurt. Though I appeared composed, deep down I was still that little girl longing to be seen and heard.

During adolescence, I longed for love and a deeper sense of belonging, even though I felt connected in my home environment. At twenty-one, I became a mother to three children—Randall, Brandy, and Britney— and was determined to create a loving and secure home for them. Yet beneath that commitment, I carried scars from my own unprocessed experiences.

Without realizing it, I clung to roles that helped me survive: the strong mother, the polished professional, the faithful churchgoer. These roles helped me look put together on the outside while I continued to hide the fear, pain, and uncertainty within.

Over time, these masks became barriers. I obsessed over perfection, battled constant self-criticism, and avoided emotional vulnerability. I appeared stable, but I was merely functioning and not thriving. I kept busy but never felt truly fulfilled.

I brought that emotional weight into motherhood, parenting from a place of both love and unhealed pain. My past began shaping my reactions, expectations, and my connection with my children. The words I used, the way I disciplined, and how I expressed affection were all influenced by wounds I had not yet confronted.

I vividly remember moments when the burden of those scars felt overwhelming. As a young mother, I often struggled with feelings of unworthiness. My attempts to be the "perfect" mom were driven by a deep fear of inadequacy. I overcompensated with structure and discipline, while inside I longed for connection and security. The harder I tried to appear strong, the more evident it became that I was still carrying a wounded identity.

It took time and God's gentle grace to help me see that my striving for control was really a cry for security. I wasn't a bad mother; I was a hurting one, trying to give what I had never fully received. As I began facing my past instead of hiding from it, I learned that healing doesn't erase the story; it redeems it.

Breaking those cycles wasn't just about changing behavior. It meant inviting God to uncover the roots beneath my patterns and to heal what I had long buried. As Psalm 51:6 says, "You desire truth in the inward parts." When I surrendered to that truth, the journey toward freedom and transformation began.

For years, I tried to manage my pain through external strength, but healing started when I finally let God into the places I had kept guarded. Through prayer, journaling, and the support of wise counsel, I began to see myself through His eyes—whole, worthy, and deeply loved. As I leaned into the process, I found peace in releasing the burdens I had carried for so long. The emotional residue that once shaped my thoughts began to lose its grip.

But the work of healing was brutal at times. It required sitting with wounds I had buried, including memories of abandonment, rejection, unmet emotional needs, and traumatic experiences that had shaped the way I saw myself and the world around me. I had to face how those experiences had shaped my relationships, my reactions, and my motherhood. It was painful, but it was necessary. What we don't confront, we continue to carry. And I was tired of carrying pain I no longer needed to bear.

As I healed, I saw shifts in how I parented and connected with others. I became more patient, more present, more compassionate. I gave my children permission to express their feelings without fear. For the first time, I modeled vulnerability and showed them that healing is possible. This new way of living wasn't perfect, but it was real. And it was rooted in grace, not performance.

Healing is not a destination. It is a continuous journey that calls for patience, faith, and the courage to remain open. Even now, memories sometimes resurface, but they no longer define me. The scars they left behind are no longer signs of brokenness. They are reminders of God's power to restore what was once shattered. Each scar tells a story of survival, resilience, and grace.

Our past may try to shape us, but it does not have the authority to define who we become. When I surrendered the residue of my childhood wounds to God, He exchanged my pain for peace and turned my deepest wounds into purpose. His grace didn't just soothe my scars; it transformed my heart and renewed my mind. As 2 Corinthians 5:17 reminds us, "If anyone is in Christ, he is a new creation; the old has gone, the new has come." The hidden wounds I once buried had tried to write the narrative of my life, whispering lies about my worth and identity.

But as I leaned into the voice of the Holy Spirit and chose to walk with intention, I came to understand that even my broken pieces were part of God's design. What once felt like ruin was being rebuilt into the very foundation of my calling and destiny.

As a project manager, I'm wired to chase results: short sprints, clear outcomes, and tangible progress. But healing doesn't follow that rhythm. It's not fast. It's not tidy. It's more like a marathon through thick fog, each step requiring courage, even when you can't see what's ahead. Some days, you move forward; other days, it feels like you're falling apart. Yet that breaking is part of the becoming. Healing unfolds in layers, in silence, in the unseen places where God does His deepest work. And then, without warning, something shifts. Truth rises to the surface. Light breaks through. That's the moment when everything starts to make sense, the light bulb moment that helps you see more clearly as you continue the journey.

If you find yourself burdened by hidden scars, know that you are not alone. Healing begins when you invite truth into your heart, allowing God to illuminate the areas you have kept hidden. By confronting these scars with courage and faith, you can begin to rewrite the narrative that once defined you.

To begin this process, here are a few steps I would like to share:

Reflect: *Start journaling about past moments that still feel unresolved. Write freely. Do not judge your emotions, just let them come.*

Pray: *Ask God to reveal the hidden places in your heart. Invite Him into your healing process.*

Seek Community: *Healing rarely happens in isolation. Speak to a trusted friend, counselor, or mentor who can walk with you.*

Find Scripture: *Meditate on verses like Psalm 34:18 ("The Lord is close to the brokenhearted"), and Isaiah 61:1 ("He has sent me to bind up the brokenhearted")*

Be Kind to Yourself: *Remember, healing is not linear. There will be good days and hard days. Extend grace to yourself in the process.*

Reflection Questions:

1. Are there any unresolved wounds or childhood experiences that may influence how you respond to others today?

2. What masks do you find yourself wearing to hide pain, insecurity, or fear? What would it look like to take those masks off?

_____

_____

_____

_____

_____

3. How might inviting God into those hidden places of your heart change the way you see yourself and others?

_____

_____

_____

_____

_____

—— Chapter 2 ——

LIGHT BULB MOMENTS

ILLUMINATION ON THE PATH

E very journey has defining moments—turning points that bring clarity, awaken understanding, and inspire transformation. In parenting, these "light bulb moments" often arrive unannounced, breaking through the monotony of routine

and revealing profound truths not just about our children, but about ourselves. They are divine insights, revelations that challenge us, humble us, and change us.

Although I was raised in church, my early understanding of faith was shaped more by my mother's belief than by a personal relationship with God. But at 21, something began to shift. A quiet but powerful spiritual awakening broke through the emotional walls I had carefully built. God's love reached places within me that had been closed off for years. That moment marked the beginning of a new chapter, and a reordering of priorities, even though pain still lingered beneath the surface.

Yet even amid that shift, I felt an unshakable yearning—a deep desire to know God for myself. I could sense His presence, and with it came a growing hunger to understand who I was in Christ. My heart began to change in ways I couldn't fully explain. Where confusion once clouded my view, clarity broke through like morning light. An undeniable longing stirred within me, not just to learn about God, but to truly encounter Him and cultivate an authentic, life-transforming relationship that was mine alone.

The following year, I met Granvell. At the time, my youngest child was only six months old. Three years later, we were married, a beautiful new beginning filled with hope and promise. After we married, we decided it would be best for Randall, Brandy, and Britney to call him "Dad." Though their biological father remained somewhat present, Granvell had stepped into that role in our home, offering stability, love, and guidance. Marrying him was one of the greatest decisions I ever made, yet it also brought old wounds to the surface. My faith was still growing, but my trauma remained unresolved. I hadn't yet faced the pain buried deep within me, and it wasn't long before those hidden wounds began to influence my marriage, affect my children, and distort my sense of identity.

One moment I'll never forget was when my son quietly said, "Mom, I get scared when you're mad." He wasn't being disrespectful or defiant—he was simply being honest. His words pierced my heart and stripped away my defenses. In that instant, I realized that my healing wasn't just important; it was necessary for the emotional safety and well-being of my children.

Parenting from a place of unhealed pain causes harm, even when we mean well. I was reactive, short-tempered, and emotionally distant at times. But light bulb moments brought truth, and truth became the catalyst for change.

Coming out of the broken cycles I described in Chapter One; I began to understand that true healing wasn't just about repairing the past. It was also about learning to be fully present in the moment. The experiences that shifted me the most weren't loud or dramatic; they were quiet, nudges—subtle ways God opened my eyes to truths I had previously overlooked. The change didn't happen all at once. But over time, my heart began to soften, and with that softening came a noticeable shift in my behavior. My responses grew gentler, my tone became more thoughtful, and my presence felt more anchored in grace. It wasn't a sudden transformation. Rather, it was a gradual and steady process of renewal, a journey of inner change that slowly began to reshape how I showed up in the world.

As my heart began to change, so did my home. The atmosphere became more peaceful. My responses grew gentler, and my tone no longer carried the harshness or intensity it once did. Love became less about fixing and more about simply being real with God—asking Him to help me and to show me how to love the way He does.

I stopped praying for God to change the people around me and began asking Him to change me. Therapy became a safe space where I could explore the roots of my emotions—the why behind my reactions, the childhood wounds I had buried, and the patterns I had unknowingly repeated. It helped me connect the dots between my past and my present, giving language to pain I had long silenced.

Journaling became one of my greatest tools. Each page revealed buried truths and hidden progress. Looking back at past entries reminded me how far I'd come—even when I didn't feel it. Writing allowed me to partner with God in uncovering what needed healing and celebrating what He was restoring.

Prayer was no longer just a desperate cry for rescue; it became my daily lifeline, anchoring me in God's presence as He guided me through the process of healing. It was in the quiet, consistent rhythm of therapy, journaling, and spending time with God—even if only ten minutes, as long as it was quality time—that He began rewriting the story I believed about myself and reshaping the way I showed up in the lives of those I loved.

Granvell's steady love became a living reflection of God's patience with me. As I began to open up and share my struggles, I discovered that vulnerability built bridges between us. Where I once feared rejection, I instead found deeper intimacy. His consistent, compassionate, and unwavering presence reminded me of God's goodness.

Emotionally, I was still unraveling. I used to joke with my sister, Auanita, saying, "I would have left me a long time ago." But Granvell never did. His love didn't flinch in the face of my mess. It stayed constant, even while I was still searching for healing and learning how to love myself.

These moments of awakening weren't just for me; they were for the legacy I longed to leave. They reminded me that parenting isn't about perfection, it's about presence. It's about trusting God to work through our brokenness to build something purposeful and lasting.

If you're yearning for change, ask God to open your eyes and reveal what needs healing. When that revelation comes, lean in. Those light bulb moments could be the very turning point that leads you into the life and legacy you were created for. Remember, God doesn't reveal these things to shame you. He reveals them because He sees beyond the pain. He sees the real you—the one He designed with purpose— and He is inviting you into healing and wholeness. *"Before I formed you in the womb, I knew you, before you were born, I set you apart…"*
—Jeremiah 1:5 (NIV)

With time and reflection, I've come to realize these awakenings were never random. Each one was a divine invitation, God's way of gently preparing my heart. He was laying a foundation of trust, calling me to surrender, and building the kind of faith I would need to parent from a place of love instead of fear. Every light bulb moment illuminated the next step in my journey, guiding me out of survival mode and into spiritual alignment.

What followed was a season of sowing. I planted spiritual seeds with faith, nurtured them through prayer, and believed that transformation was quietly taking root—not just in my children, but in me. I learned to trust that what is planted in faith will bloom in God's perfect time. As I continued to grow in His Word, I came to understand that healing isn't just about the past; it's about building a legacy of wholeness for generations to come.

Reflection Questions:

1. Have you experienced any "light bulb moments" in your parenting or personal growth that shifted your perspective or response?

2. In what ways might you be parenting or reacting from unhealed pain? What would it look like to invite God into that space?

_____

_____

_____

_____

_____

3. How can you begin planting seeds of grace, presence, and emotional safety in your relationships today?

_____

_____

_____

_____

_____

—— Chapter 3 ——

PLANTING SEEDS OF FAITH

TRUSTING GOD IN THE EARLY YEARS

As a parent, one of the hardest lessons I've had to learn is how to embrace God's timing—especially when it comes to my children. In the early years, I believed that if I poured in enough love, wisdom, and guidance, I would quickly see the fruit of my efforts.

Yet parenting calls for a deeper kind of faith. It believes God is doing unseen work in our children's hearts, shaping their paths and guiding their steps long before we see the evidence with our own eyes.

During those early years, my husband and I worked tirelessly to create a stable, faith-filled home. We taught and modeled Christian values, knowing we weren't perfect but striving to point our children to the

One who is. There were times we argued in front of them, moments when stress and exhaustion got the best of us. Still, we always returned to what mattered most—love, forgiveness, and faith in God.

We could not control every detail of our children's lives, but we could be faithful in planting seeds of love, compassion, discipline, integrity, and spiritual grounding. And so, we did just that, day after day, in small and intentional ways. Our Christian values were not just lip service; we did our best to live them. Church attendance was not optional. Sunday mornings and Wednesday nights became meaningful rhythms of life, grounding us in faith rather than mere routine. These moments were opportunities for our children to grow spiritually, build relationships with other believers, and see firsthand that our commitment to God was central to everything.

We made it a priority to instill Christian values at home, drawing on the faith traditions we were raised with and carrying those roots into our parenting. We taught the importance of hard work, honesty, showing grace, and extending kindness—even when it wasn't easy.

Our children were watching, even when we didn't realize it. Every word spoken, every action taken, became a silent lesson shaping their understanding of what it means to live with integrity and faith.

Life was full and demanding. With both of us working full-time and raising three children, our days rarely slowed down. Mornings felt like a daily marathon: waking the kids, getting them dressed, packing their bags, and rushing out the door to daycare and work. Every moment was a race against the clock, leaving little time to pause or catch our breath.

Evenings brought another round of activity with homework, dinner, and preparing for the next day. Yet, amid all the busyness, we made room to notice and nurture the unique gifts God had given to Randall, Brandy, and Britney.

In the midst of tight schedules and limited resources, we tried to keep them connected to positive, meaningful activities. Both of our daughters were enrolled in dance classes, though only one truly enjoyed it, while our son, Randall, had a creative spark that showed up in art and drama. We encouraged his gifts by enrolling him in art classes and acting lessons, which brought him so much joy.

In hindsight, I wish I had done more to nurture Brandy's gift for singing. Her voice was so pure and full of emotion. I wish I had encouraged Brandy's love for singing more intentionally. I regret not creating space earlier to nurture that gift.

At the time, I chose what was convenient, keeping both girls in the same dance class, rather than making a thoughtful, individualized decision. I didn't fully grasp the importance of that choice then. When Brandy got older, I eventually enrolled her in singing lessons, but by that time, I think the spark had already faded. That realization still tugs at my heart, because as parents, we should give our children every opportunity to thrive in what they love, even when it isn't the most convenient.

Parents, be encouraged: if you see talents and giftings in your children at a young age, nurture them. As Proverbs 18:16 reminds us, "A person's gift makes room for him", so allow their gifts to flourish, even though it may require sacrifices both financially and with your time. Those investments, though costly in the moment, can help shape their confidence and future.

Along with supporting their gifts, we also treasured the everyday moments that kept us close as a family. One of the most meaningful was gathering around the dinner table. The food didn't need to be fancy; the connection was what mattered. We prayed, laughed, shared about the day, and comforted each other. That table became the heart of our home, a place of refuge and connection.

Out of those family meals grew a tradition we called 'VIP Dinner.' Whenever one of the children had a standout moment, whether earning a good grade, showing kindness, or overcoming a challenge in school, they were celebrated at the table.

Brandy and Britney were crowned 'Queen for the Evening,' and Randall was honored as 'King for the Evening.' We set the table with fine China, giving them a special plate and silverware to mark the occasion. The whole family joined in to celebrate, turning an ordinary meal into a moment of affirmation. It was our way of teaching them that effort, character, and perseverance were just as worthy of honor as achievement.

More importantly, it reminded them that God values the heart above accomplishments, and that character is always worth celebrating. These intentional traditions reinforced what we believed: each of them matters, every effort counts, and love is shown in both big and small ways. We loved this celebration because it was also a reminder to slow down and appreciate progress. In this digital world, where distractions often pull families apart, my hope is that others can discover the joy of pausing to honor the little victories that matter so much, or even create their own rendition of a tradition that speaks love into their home.

I often found myself holding tightly to Proverbs 22:6: "Train up a child in the way he should go, and when he is old, he will not depart from it." That verse became more than words on a page; it was a promise I leaned on in the thick of parenting. I whispered prayers over my children as they slept, asking God to cover them. I read Bible verses aloud at the table or before bedtime, sometimes wondering if they were really listening. I offered forgiveness when tempers flared and tried to use everyday moments as teaching opportunities.

Deep down, I trusted that even the smallest seeds we planted mattered, and that God was at work in their hearts, even when I couldn't see the fruit yet. Still, there were nights I lay awake, questioning if we were doing enough. What if they rejected everything we worked so hard to build? But then I remembered my own journey. I had wandered from the faith my mother taught me. I had rebelled, searched, and wrestled with my own path.

And yet, because of the seeds she planted, I found my way back not just to the lessons she taught me, but to a loving God who saved me. The truth she sowed in my heart never let me go. It was not forced or demanded; it was faith taking root and becoming real in my own life, in God's perfect timing.

For every parent who wonders if their efforts are enough, take heart: when God's Word is planted in love, it will bear fruit in His time. As Isaiah 55:11 promises, His Word never returns empty. Be encouraged, every prayer, every act of love, and every seed of truth you plant is being used by God to shape a harvest you may not see yet, but one He is faithfully bringing to pass.

Through those years, I learned that trusting God in parenting doesn't mean thoughts of worry won't come to try to steal your peace; it means returning again and again to the One who loves our children more than we do. Parenting isn't about control; it's about stewardship. We plant. We water. We pray. And we trust God to do what only He can do.

Reflection for Parents

To every parent who wonders if it matters: it does.

Your love matters. Your words matter. Your presence matters.

Keep planting. Keep praying. Keep believing. One day, the seeds you've sown will bloom in ways you never imagined, and it will all be worth it.

Still, the time came when the seeds we had planted were tested by storms we didn't see coming. The early structure gave way to teenage seasons of change, questions, and pulling away. It was in this new stretch of parenting, where letting go became harder than holding on, that my trust in God was deepened most as I continued to walk through the journey and process of parenting.

Reflection Questions:

1. What seeds of faith and character are you intentionally planting in your children or those you influence?

_____

_____

_____

_____

_____

2. In what ways are you tempted to control outcomes, and how might God be inviting you to trust Him more?

_____

_____

_____

_____

_____

3. Are there any past experiences where you saw God bring fruit from seeds planted long ago? How can those memories strengthen your faith today?

_____

_____

_____

_____

_____

—— Chapter 4 ——

THE ADOLESCENT SHIFT

TRUSTING GOD THROUGH THE STORM OF CHANGE

■ ■ ■ ■ ────────────────────────────

Adolescence is a pivotal stage in a child's life, a season of transition marked by growth, self-discovery, and challenges. For parents, it can feel like stepping into unfamiliar territory. The sweet innocence of childhood gives way to the

complexities of teenagers navigating independence, identity, and peer influence. It's a time when both children and parents are stretched in ways they never imagined.

It is also a time of rapid physical, emotional, and psychological changes. Teenagers begin to seek independence, develop their sense of identity, and strive for autonomy. They may push boundaries, challenge authority, and wrestle with peer pressure while navigating the uncertainties of who they are and where they belong.

This stage often comes with heightened emotions, a desire for privacy, and a yearning for acceptance. Adolescents want to feel heard and understood, but they may struggle to articulate their needs. They crave freedom, yet they still need the security and guidance of their parents. It's a delicate balance that can feel like walking a tightrope for both the child and the parent.

As children enter these years, they begin to shape their own views of the world, often questioning the beliefs and values they were raised with. This process of exploration is a natural and necessary part of their development, but it can feel unsettling for parents who are used to having more influence in their children's decisions. Suddenly, the dynamics within the home begin to shift, and the strategies that once worked no longer seem as effective. Parenting during adolescence often demands a deeper level of patience, understanding, and grace— qualities I didn't always possess, but ones I've grown into over time.

Just when I thought I had found my footing in one season of parenting, a new chapter began, one that felt even more unfamiliar and demanding. Parenting adolescents brought challenges I wasn't fully prepared for, and one of the hardest parts was living with the weight of uncertainty. Their choices, their struggles, and even their mistakes often felt like a reflection of my own parenting, which left me wrestling with guilt and self-doubt.

During those adolescent years, I didn't recognize this part of the journey as a gift. The whirlwind of defiance and uncertainty often left me feeling unanchored. I was often overwhelmed, frustrated, and riddled with anxiety. There were moments when it felt like the world was closing in, especially during times when they disrespected me or Granvell. Some of their words were so cold they pierced straight through, leaving me questioning where I had gone wrong. Had I failed them somehow? Had all the seeds I planted fallen on hard soil? I remember lying awake at night, wondering if this cycle of pain, rebellion, and distance would ever end or if I'd forever be stuck in a loop trying to fix what felt so broken.

I vividly remember one incident with my son, Randall. He had disrespected Granvell in a way that left us both stunned. The words he said shocked us, and in the heat of the moment, Granvell told him to leave the house. I was left feeling confused, upset, and caught in the middle of their feud. All I wanted was peace in my home and my family to be together, but instead, it felt like everything was falling apart.

That night, as my marriage felt strained and uncertain, I wrestled with a storm of emotions. We were no longer aligned, our hearts moving in different directions. The next evening, around 11 p.m., Randall called and asked if I could come pick him up. I told him he needed to call his father, Granvell. When Granvell arrived, not a single word passed between them. The silence in the car only deepened his frustration, and by the time they returned home, his anger was evident. Granvell looked at me with a cold intensity and said words that shattered my heart: "I'll have mercy on him tonight, but tomorrow he's out of here.

Hearing those words, I felt completely undone. I immediately cried out to the Lord, "Help me! I'm drowning!" I was angry with my son for disrespecting his dad, and with my husband for how he was handling the situation. The weight of it all crushed me in ways I couldn't put into words.

I knew I needed to get alone with God. For once, I didn't come to Him with a list of requests; I simply poured out my heart. I shared with Him my frustration, my hurt, and my fears. I opened my journal and wrote about the incident, releasing everything onto the page. As I wrote, the words began to flow, raw and unfiltered. I ended with a simple but desperate plea: "God, I love You, and I'm not leaving You."

That moment of surrender didn't solve all my problems, but it gave me a sense of release. It reminded me that I wasn't alone in the storm. God was with me, even in the messiness of my family's struggles. He saw my pain, heard my cries, and held me as I navigated the chaos of adolescence and the strain it brought to my marriage.

As a mother, one of my deepest fears during my children's adolescent years was seeing them attracted to people or situations that I knew could lead them down a dangerous path. This fear became very real when I noticed one of my daughters showing interest in boys who were involved in street life. Street life refers to the lifestyle and experiences of individuals who spend much of their time navigating the challenges of survival-based hustling, and may sometimes involve illegal activity.

I saw the subtle signs: her change in demeanor, the way she would light up when she mentioned their names, and how she seemed to be pulled toward the allure of rebellion. I tried to talk to her, to warn her, but my words fell on deaf ears. Adolescents have a way of seeing only the excitement and not the consequences. My heart ached as I watched her make choices that I knew could lead to heartbreak or worse. I remember one specific evening when I saw my daughter walking home with one of the boys I had been warning her about. My heart sank. I wanted to run out and pull her away, to demand she come home and never speak to him again. But I knew that approach would only lead to more rebellion and possibly push her closer to him. Instead, I prayed. I stood at the window and whispered, "Lord, open her eyes. Let her see the truth about the path she's walking down before it's too late."

That night, I could see the defensiveness in her eyes. She knew I wasn't happy. But instead of reacting in anger, I simply hugged her. It wasn't what she expected, and I could feel her hesitation. I told her I loved her and that I wanted the best for her—even if she didn't always understand my concern. That moment opened a door. It didn't solve everything, but it softened her heart.

With my other daughter, I had to rely on God for wisdom. She was always quieter and more private, and deep down, I sensed she might have been involved in her own mischief. Whatever she was doing, she kept it hidden from me. There were moments when I noticed subtle clues, a suspicious look, or a vague answer, but nothing concrete enough to confront. One day, I found a note tucked into her school bag that hinted at a friendship I had concerns about. Instead of reacting with suspicion, I prayed for the right words and approach. When I gently brought it up, she shared more than I anticipated, revealing a side of her I hadn't seen before. She admitted to spending time with people who weren't a good influence and confessed that she wasn't proud of some of the choices she had made.

During those years, my prayers were mostly about protection, as my children began making more of their own choices and spending much of their time with friends. In their mid-teens, new challenges emerged as they learned to drive, tested boundaries further, and gained greater independence. My prayers deepened during that time, asking God to give them wisdom and keep them safe from negative influences. Though that season held many joyful moments, it also brought nights of tears and quiet talks with God as worry filled my heart. I didn't always surrender those fears to Him and often held on to them longer than I should have. Some days, I believed with confidence; other days, fear crept in and clouded my vision.

Slowly, I began learning to meditate on His Word again and to turn to Scripture for peace. I think what made that season especially difficult was how often I wrestled with trust. I came to understand that trust isn't a one-time decision; it's a daily choice to let go of control and believe that God is still working behind the scenes. I was learning that trust didn't mean having all the answers. It meant leaning into God even when everything felt uncertain.

As I spent more time in His presence, I clung to the hope that the seeds I had planted in my children, seeds of God's Word, would one day take root and bear fruit, even if I couldn't see it at the time.

That slow process began to reshape me, not because I had reached unshakable faith, but because I kept returning to God in my weakness. I chose, moment by moment, to release control and quiet my anxious thoughts, sometimes trembling, yet trusting that He was still writing their story. I kept renewing my mind, asking God to help me believe again as I declared God's truth about my children and that His promises still stood and His faithfulness was at work in the waiting.

Reflecting on those years, I can see just how much I wrestled with fear, frustration, and the overwhelming urge to control. I wanted to shield Randall, Brandy, and Britney from every mistake, harmful influence, and painful consequence. My heart ached with a deep longing to protect them from hurt, but adolescence confronted me with a hard truth: I couldn't control their choices. I had to let go of the illusion that I could protect them from every mistake or bad decision. I could only guide them, cover them in prayer, and trust that God would meet them exactly where they were. Letting go little by little wasn't a sign of weakness; it was a courageous act of faith. In that surrender, I discovered a strength I didn't know I had. Trusting God with their hearts became a daily decision, and over time, I realized it was one of the greatest expressions of love I could give. Adolescence was not just a storm my children had to navigate; it was a season that tested my own faith as a mother.

Overall, I learned that the most powerful thing I could do for my children was to be present, to listen, and to pray. In the process, I discovered a precious gift, the realization that God was shaping me through every season of their growth. What I once saw as chaos became the very place where patience, surrender, and faith took root. It's a lesson I carry with me even now, knowing that the storms of adolescence, though painful, were also the soil in which deeper faith grew in me and in which a deeper trust in God's plan for their journey was embraced.

As the winds calmed, a new horizon came into view. The complexity of parenting adult children brought a different kind of challenge. As each of them left the nest to begin their own journeys and make their own decisions, my role began to shift. I was no longer managing curfews or refereeing disagreements. Instead, I found myself praying over life choices, career directions, relationships, and spiritual grounding.

Reflection Questions:

1. When my child's choices challenge my values or expectations, do I respond with control, fear, or trust? What might surrendering that moment to God look like in practice?

2. How have the struggles and uncertainties of my child's adolescence deepened my faith or exposed areas where I need to grow in patience, empathy, or grace?

3. In what ways can I shift from trying to fix or protect my children to instead guiding, praying, and trusting God to shape their hearts in His timing?

—— Chapter 5 ——

WHEN THEY LEAVE THE NEST

WATCHING FROM THE SIDELINES

■ ■ ■ ■ ─────────────────────────────

A s each of our children began to stretch their wings and make decisions beyond our reach, I realized that parenting wasn't ending; it was transforming. The role I once held on the frontlines, guiding, correcting, and protecting, was slowly giving way to a quieter role of intercession and deeper trust. I could no longer control the outcomes of their choices or shield them from every consequence, and that realization brought both fear and freedom. It was in that letting go that I learned to lean on God in a new way, not just to ask Him to fix things, but to truly trust Him with their lives. Little did I know that I would retreat from trust when fear whispered louder than faith. There were moments I found myself trying to take back what I had surrendered, clinging to control out of worry and love. Yet even in those moments,

God was patient, gently reminding me that His hands were stronger than mine. Over time, I began to understand that my greatest act of love was not holding on tighter, but releasing them fully into His care, believing that the same God who carried me would also carry them.

I once believed that launching my children into adulthood would feel like a long-awaited milestone. I pictured peace and fulfillment, knowing I had given them all I could: my faith, my love, my guidance, and that it was their turn to fly.

But stepping back proved far harder than I imagined. I was still growing in this aspect of learning how to support without rescuing and love without controlling. It wasn't easy to step back, but it was necessary. Watching them make choices that sometimes brought pain was heartbreaking. The shift from active parenting to quiet sideline support carried an ache I didn't expect, the ache of distance, of not knowing, of seeing them walk paths that went against so much of what I had poured into them.

For years, I held their hands, guided their steps, and covered them in prayer. Then, almost without warning, my hands were no longer guiding but letting go. The house grew quiet, and my prayers turned into whispers from afar. Eventually, all three of my children left the nest. A coworker once told me, "You've given them wings. Now they have to learn how to fly." Those words stayed with me. Letting go wasn't failure; it was trust.

Like many parents, I had high hopes for my children's futures. I wanted them to chase their dreams, pursue their passions, and reach their God-given potential. I thought my three biological children would break the poverty curse in our family so that, together, we could finally help others accomplish their goals.

We even took a leap of faith and relocated to California, believing this would be the catalyst for generational change. We poured ourselves into building a new life, trusting that the fresh environment would open doors for our children to flourish. But the story that unfolded wasn't as tidy as I had envisioned. It was complicated, raw, and deeply humbling. It marked the beginning of a different kind of faith, a faith that relied not on my parenting but on God's sovereignty.

Parenting adult children is a delicate dance between offering support and staying silent. Silence came naturally to my husband, but not to me. I believed that if I just kept talking, they would understand. I was wrong. I had to learn that they must take ownership of their choices, and as much as I wanted to shield them from hardship, their lives were now in their hands and ultimately in God's.

Both my husband and I now have a deeper understanding of what our parents must have felt when they stayed up late, praying for us. These days, when worry tries to take hold, I turn to God's promises. As 1 Peter 5:7 reminds us, *"Cast all your anxiety on him because he cares for you."* And Philippians 4:6–7 strengthens me to trade worry for prayer: *"Do not be anxious about anything, but in every situation, by prayer and petition, with thanksgiving, present your requests to God. And the peace of God, which transcends all understanding, will guard your hearts and your minds in Christ Jesus."*

That peace reminds me that a parent's love doesn't diminish with distance; it deepens. It becomes a guiding light that gently calls our children back to truth and purpose. As Psalm 31:15 declares, *"My times are in your hands."* I hold fast to this promise, trusting that my children's times, every season and every moment, are in God's hands.

Still, trusting didn't mean I failed to notice the changes. I remember the slow unraveling, the kind I could see only when I was paying close attention. One of my children, once so full of joy, began to change. It wasn't dramatic, but little by little through friendships, posture, and tone, I watched their light dim.

One night, they came home at 2 a.m. Something was different. Their spirit felt muted, withdrawn. I tried to stay calm, but inside I was bracing myself. Push too hard and I risk being shut out. Say nothing, and I might seem indifferent. That tension was agonizing.

In that moment, I realized how delicate the balance had become. I was no longer the parent who could fix everything with a hug, a prayer at the bedside, or a word of guidance. Now I had to hold my tongue, guard my reactions, and trust that God would do what I could not. My heart longed to reach in and rescue, yet I knew love sometimes meant waiting in the shadows, praying unseen, and believing that God's hand was still at work even when I couldn't see the evidence.

Those years brought many such moments: the early morning phone calls that made my heart pound, the news of driving under the influence, domestic violence incidents, and emergencies that left me breathless and praying for mercy. These weren't just disruptions to my sleep; they were sobering reminders of how far life had shifted from the future I once pictured for my children.

The most painful part was watching my children invest in people and pursuits that drained them. One relationship in particular broke my heart. I watched as it diminished my child's confidence and joy, leaving a shadow where there once was light. I wanted to intervene, to protect, to rescue, but transformation had to come from within them and in God's timing.

So, I prayed. I prayed for their eyes to be opened, for their hearts to be shielded, for God to do what I could not. In time, the veil lifted, but not without cost. Lessons came with pain. Healing came, but it carried scars.

After some years in California, a shift came. One child moved to Texas, one stayed in California but faced battles of their own, and another returned to Delaware. I questioned everything. Had we done enough? Was moving to California a mistake? The dreams we chased felt fractured. I wrestled not with my children, but with God, struggling to surrender my expectations and trust His plan.

When I saw my children in unfulfilling jobs, my instinct was to step in with advice. But advice so often turned into lectures, and lecturing became my default response. I thought if I just kept talking, explaining, reminding, and pushing, they would finally "get it" and make different choices. Deep down, I believed my words could redirect their steps. But all my talking often left them feeling criticized instead of encouraged, and me feeling frustrated that nothing was changing.

Even as I tried to affirm, I still slipped back into old habits. In time, I began to see that what they needed wasn't another speech. They needed affirmation. So, I started small. Instead of pointing out what was wrong, I reminded them of their gifts, their talents, their worth. Slowly, I began to see flickers of hope as they started to believe in themselves again.

That was also when I realized one of the hardest things: my fixing wasn't always helping. As a project manager, being a fixer has always been my strength. I could line up resources, mitigate risks, and push projects to the finish line. But with my children, my fixing and lecturing sometimes pushed them further away rather than drawing them closer.

One of my daughters felt this most deeply. She told me that my quick interventions made her feel I didn't trust her as a mother. The advice I offered with good intentions often landed as criticism. It took courage to invite my children into honest conversations and ask, "Do I come across as overbearing or controlling?" Their answers were hard to hear, but they opened my eyes.

During this season, it taught me to shift from fixer to faithful intercessor. I failed at this many times, trying to control outcomes or fix problems in my own strength. Eventually, I began to understand the power of presence and prayer. I learned how to offer choices instead of giving my opinionated advice or starting with, "I think you should…" Now, when my children share their struggles, I pause and ask, "Do you want advice, or do you just want me to listen?" I try to offer choices rather than give commands. And above all, I pray first.

This approach has given me peace. I am still growing and still learning to let go. When the urge to control rises, I pause and breathe, reminding myself that God is at work in their lives just as He is in mine. That awareness makes room for grace, the kind that softens the heart and opens the door to forgiveness. Over time, I've come to understand that forgiveness isn't just a one- time decision. It's a process that opens the door to real healing.

As a mother, I didn't always recognize the ways I may have hurt my children, whether through words spoken in exhaustion, moments I missed, or attempts to control what I should have simply entrusted to God. At the same time, my children didn't always see the wounds they left in me. Sometimes it was in the words they said. Sometimes in silence. And other times, in choices that felt like rejection.

But healing began when I humbled myself before God. I asked Him to forgive me for the things I did and for the things I overlooked. I confessed my failures, my missteps, and the times I let frustration speak louder than love.

Then came the moment that would begin my own healing. I chose to forgive my children. I released the pain of words that cut deep, the seasons of distance, and the moments they hurt me, whether they realized it or not. Forgiveness did not erase the pain, but it broke the heavy chains of resentment I hadn't realized I was carrying. Grace found space to move freely. Love sank its roots deeper into the soil of my heart, and reconciliation began its quiet, steady work. My heart began to heal.

Sometimes, when I look at my children through my own limited perspective, I wonder why they aren't further along in their spiritual journey. I see the gap, the space between where they are and where I had hoped they would be by now. I notice the choices that don't reflect what I've taught them, the lack of interest in spiritual things, and the distractions that seem to pull their hearts in other directions. It stirs something in me, a desire to fix it, to speed up their growth, to steer them toward what I believe is best.

But then I pause and remind myself that I'm only seeing part of the story. My view is shaped by human expectations and emotions. That's when I turn to the truth of Psalm 31:15: *"My times are in Your hands."* And not just my time, but theirs too. Every moment of their past, every step of their present, and every hope for their future is already held in God's capable hands.

He sees the full picture. Every delay, detour, and decision is part of a greater plan. He is still working, even when I can't see the progress.

That truth brings me peace. I don't have to carry the burden of their spiritual journey alone. I can release them again and again into the hands of a loving God who knows them deeply and loves them even more than I do.

I share this part of my journey so that you know you are not walking this road alone. Letting go is never easy, but it is part of the faith walk. It is where we keep learning to trust, where love meets surrender, and where we release our grip and remember that we were never meant to be Saviors. That role belongs to Jesus, and He is faithful.

In the next chapter, you will hear from two women who, like me, have faced the painful yet freeing process of releasing their children to God. Their stories reflect different paths but the same divine thread of grace and trust. As you read their journeys, may you find comfort, strength, and the gentle reminder that God's grace meets you right where you are.

Reflection Questions

1. Where in my parenting am I tempted to step in and "fix" when I should pause, pray, and wait?

_____

_____

_____

_____

2. Are there areas where I have held on too tightly to how I thought my children's lives should unfold, rather than allowing God to lead their path?

_____

_____

_____

_____

3. In what ways has my role as a parent changed now that my children are adults? How am I navigating that shift?

_____

_____

_____

_____

_____

—— Chapter 6 ——

STORIES FROM THE JOURNEY

FINDING STRENGHT IN THE RELEASE

■ ■ ■ ■ ────────────────────────

From Pastor Sonja Carter

I chose to share A Mother's Journey Through Faith and Unconditional Love first, so you can see this experience through my eyes, what I felt, prayed, and learned as a parent. My daughter's testimony follows, showing how God answered in His perfect timing. Together, our stories reveal the power of faith and transformation.

Since writing this letter my daughter's life has been transformed for 4 years now by the power of God. The chains of deception have been broken, and she is now pursuing her divine calling with boldness and humility. This moment of honesty marked the beginning of a beautiful healing journey- one rooted in truth, led by grace, and fueled by purpose.

To God Be the Glory!

For 17 years, my daughter lived a Lesbian lifestyle. As her mother, I felt deeply embarrassed, ashamed, and guilty.

I was embarrassed because I was a Christian and a minister in my church, and I did not like her behavior, nor the way she dressed, because it was very masculine. I felt ashamed because I believed her choices reflected poorly on me as a parent. I also carried guilt because when I was pregnant, I desperately wanted her to be a boy, and I feared that desire somehow influenced the path she chose.

Many nights I cried and felt completely alone. I struggled to believe God could ever transform her life. Yet in my pain, I cried out to Him. When I stopped focusing on the situation, I found moments of comfort and peace.

Even though my heart was heavy, I kept going to church, reading my Bible, and pouring out my feelings to God. Over time, He began to change me. I slowly learned to surrender control and trust Him fully. As my relationship with God grew, my mindset started to shift, and my strength became anchored in Him.

One verse became my anchor:

"Many are the plans in a man's heart, but the Lord's purpose prevails "(Proverbs 19 :21)

I chose to fix my focus on God rather than live in shame or self-pity. Even when it looked like she was drifting further away, I stood on His Word. My hope remained in His plan for her freedom.

Through it all, God strengthened my faith, healed my heart, and reminded me that His purpose is greater than any of my fears.

Letter from my daughter:

Out of Darkness into His Marvelous light." (1 Peter 2:9).

Mom,

I'm just sitting here thinking …. This spiritual warfare is real.

I just realized something God didn't create me to love a woman in that way. It's unnatural, and it's a spirit of perversion. I used to think I was gay because ever since kindergarten, I remember being attracted to girls. But now I believe that was the devil trying to plant a seed in my mind because he knew the calling God placed on my life.

From the moment I was born, the enemy knew that God was going to use me to break strongholds in women's lives, and he didn't want that to happen, so he kept planting that seed over and over again until I believed it. He doesn't want me to pray for these women; he wants me to believe that I want to be sexually involved with them to distract me from my calling.

Every woman I've ever been with has destroyed me mentally, physically, emotionally, spiritually, and financially. The devil used them to try to kill me and make me give up on God. But I don't want to believe his lies anymore. I want to remove myself from this sin. I know it won't be easy, and I may fall into temptation a few more times before I get it right, but I'm going to fight.

I don't want this life anymore. It's not pleasing in God's sight. I don't want to help the devil carry out his plan - I want to live out God's purpose for my life. I'm sick of the devil stealing from me. I know God's plan is far greater than anything I could ever dream of. No woman can ever give me the love that God has for me.

I've been reading my Bible and praying so much more. It's not about me anymore - it's about what God wants. And I want so badly to please Him. I know it's going to be rough, but I also know God can change me if I keep seeking Him.

Thank you for being the best mom ever- for walking with God and keeping me in your prayers. I truly believe God made you my mother for a reason - because He knew I would need someone as strong and God-fearing as you if I was ever going to walk in His purpose and plan for my life.

I encourage you to keep praying, seeking, and preaching His gospel. God is using you to change lives.

I love you and be blessed.

From Auanita Corley

Release: My Journey of Letting Go and Trusting God

As a teen mom, it was incredibly challenging to parent my two oldest children without the support of their fathers. I didn't mature emotionally and often bumped heads with my oldest daughter. At the time, I didn't realize I was carrying unresolved trauma. I lacked the ability to express emotions, communicate effectively, parent, nurture, and discipline in ways that offered guidance rather than shame. My mom often stepped in to provide what I could not.

When I became a Christian at the age of 20, I began taking my children to church faithfully, praying for them, and creating a home filled with rules, many of which, I now see, were rooted more in religious behavior than true relationship. What I didn't know was that there was a hole in my soul and the deep void and brokenness would affect my ability to connect with my daughter. I was still longing to be loved myself. I could only give what I had: low self-worth, limited knowledge, limited parenting skills, little patience, and a struggle to offer the love that was truly needed.

Later, I had more children, got married, and my attention shifted in that direction. Over the years, my relationship with my oldest daughter became strained. She was intelligent, beautiful, and gifted, with a 4.0 GPA and a voice that could move hearts. But her life took a difficult turn. She became addicted to prescription drugs and left home at 17.

Her journey included unstable relationships, other addictions, being homeless in Las Vegas, and years of pain and trauma.

Her outbursts of rage, anger, and blame toward me continued for years. I eventually began counseling and learned about trauma and that's when my own healing journey began. I grew in my relationship with God through Jesus Christ, and my eyes were opened. I saw how my own pain and decisions had affected how I parented. I asked for her forgiveness, but she wasn't ready. The anger and disrespect continued. I tried desperately to save her. I got seldom calls when she was experiencing panic attacks, paranoia, and mood swings. I saw my daughter in a very dark place, and I felt helpless. She was in and out of rehabs and I would still struggle with guilt and condemn myself because I felt as though this was all my fault. Not long after my mentor died, while I was grieving, my daughter exploded again in anger toward me. That day, for the first time, I spoke up, not from a place of shame or guilt, but from a place of healing and truth. I said, "I don't live there anymore." I had done the inner work. I had asked her and God for forgiveness and could no longer carry the weight of the past.

Shortly after I attended a church service, God whispered to my heart, call her once a week and love her. Even when she didn't answer, I still called and left a voicemail message, saying, "I love you," and hung up. She eventually moved out of state, changed her number, and we lost contact for a while. It hurt deeply knowing she was struggling with addiction, emotional pain, and brokenness. But all I could do was pray, love her from afar, and keep working on my own healing.

One day, out of the blue, she reached out to me while I was living in St. Augustine, FL. She asked if she could live with me. I said yes and set clear boundaries: no drugs, no disrespect, no smoking in my home. She agreed. That marked the beginning of a new chapter in our relationship. There were still setbacks, but I remained focused on my healing and my relationship with God.

Later, when I bought a home in Delaware, she moved in and began her own transformation. I witnessed her growth, maturity, and emotional healing. Today, our relationship is stronger and healthier than ever. We are building from a place of truth, grace, and love.

Reflection: How Letting Go Changed Me

Letting go didn't mean giving up on my daughter; it meant surrendering her to the One who could truly heal her. Releasing her to God allowed me to find peace, even in pain. It gave me space to grow spiritually, emotionally, and personally. It helped me stop trying to rescue and start truly trusting.

This decision deepened my faith. I learned to pray without controlling, love without conditions, and heal without waiting for someone else's apology or approval. My relationship with my daughter is still growing, and it's real. We've both changed, and God continues to do what only He can do.

Encouragement to Other Parents

To the parent who is hurting, praying, and holding on: I see you. Releasing your child does not mean you failed. It means you are learning to trust God more than you trust your fears. Surrender is hard, especially when we want to fix, rescue, or protect. But healing often happens when we step back and let God step in. For me, surrendering came in layers, not all at once.

Keep praying. Keep growing. Keep loving. And most of all, please keep your heart open to healing. Your child's story is still being written, and so is yours. You are not alone.

"Cast all your cares on Him, because He cares for you."
— 1 Peter 5:7 (CSB)

Entrusting your pain, child, and past to a loving God who sees, knows, and cares deeply.

—— Chapter 7 ——

BEYOND MY HANDS

SCRIPTURE BASED PRAYERS FOR OUR CHILDREN

■ ■ ■ ■ ————————————————————————

There comes a point in every parent's journey when our children move beyond our reach, but never beyond God's. When our words are no longer enough and our arms can't hold them through every season, God's Word becomes our anchor.

His promises become our prayers, our strength in uncertainty, and our hope in the unknown.

This chapter is your invitation to release your children into the faithful hands of God using Scripture as your guide. These verses are not just words on a page—they are spiritual tools, declarations of truth, and anchors of peace. As you read, pray, or speak these Scriptures aloud, insert your child's name(s) in the space provided. Let these promises become personal, powerful, and prophetic.

Note: Each Scripture includes a space to personalize with your child's name(s). Feel free to write one or more names depending on your family. This chapter is meant to meet you wherever you are—whether you're praying for one child, several, or even spiritual children God has entrusted to you.

Use the journaling space below each Scripture to write a prayer, a reflection, or what God is speaking to your heart. This is your sacred space to process, release, and grow.

1. Colossians 1:9

"We continually ask God to fill you with the knowledge of his will through all the wisdom and understanding that the Spirit gives." (NIV).

Prayer:

Lord, fill [insert child's name(s)] with the wisdom and understanding that only Your Spirit provides.

Journal:

_____

_____

_____

_____

_____

_____

_____

_____

_____

_____

_____

2. Proverbs 19:21

"Many are the plans in a person's heart, but it is the Lord's purpose that prevails." (NIV).

Prayer:

May Your purpose prevail in [insert child's name(s)]'s life, even above their own plans.

Journal:

---

3. Isaiah 54:13

"All your children will be taught by the Lord, and great will be their peace." (NIV).

Prayer:

Teach [insert child's name(s)] Your truth, Lord, and let Your peace reign in their hearts.

Journal:

_____

_____

_____

_____

_____

_____

_____

_____

_____

_____

_____

4. Psalm 31:15

"My times are in your hands; deliver me from the hands of my enemies, from those who pursue me." (NIV).

Prayer:

I place [insert child's name(s)] in Your hands. Protect and guide them according to Your will.

Journal:

_____

_____

_____

_____

_____

_____

_____

_____

_____

_____

_____

_____

5. Proverbs 22:6

"Start children off on the way they should go, and even when they are old, they will not turn from it." (NIV).

Prayer:

I trust that the seeds of truth planted in [insert child's name(s)] will take root and remain.

Journal:

_____

_____

_____

_____

_____

_____

_____

_____

_____

_____

_____

_____

6. Psalm 107:20

"He sent out his word and healed them; he rescued them from the grave." (NIV)

Prayer

Send Your healing Word to [insert child's name(s)], Lord, and rescue them from every pit.

Journal:

_____

_____

_____

_____

_____

_____

_____

_____

_____

_____

_____

_____

_____

7. Jeremiah 29:11

"For I know the plans I have for you,' declares the Lord, 'plans to prosper you and not to harm you, plans to give you hope and a future." *(NIV)*

Prayer

I trust Your plan for [insert child's name(s)]—plans full of hope and purpose.

Journal:

8. Philippians 1:6

"Being confident of this, that he who began a good work in you will carry it on to completion until the day of Christ Jesus." (NIV)

Prayer

Completely finish what You started in [insert child's name(s)], Lord.

Journal:

---

9. Psalm 121:7-8

"The Lord will keep you from all harm—he will watch over your life; the Lord will watch over your coming and going both now and forevermore." (NIV)

Prayer

Lord, watch over [insert child's name(s)] today and always.

Journal:

_____

_____

_____

_____

_____

_____

_____

_____

_____

_____

_____

10. Isaiah 41:10

"So do not fear, for I am with you; do not be dismayed, for I am your God. I will strengthen you and help you; I will uphold you with my righteous right hand." (NIV)

Prayer

Strengthen [insert child's name(s)] with Your righteous hand.

Journal:

11. Ephesians 3:20

"Now to him who is able to do immeasurably more than all we ask or imagine, according to his power that is at work within us." (NIV)

Prayer

Do more in [insert child's name(s)]'s life than I could ever imagine.

Journal:

---

12. Psalm 46:1

"God is our refuge and strength, an ever-present help in trouble." (NIV)

Prayer

Be [insert child's name(s)]'s refuge and strength in every season.

Journal:

_____

_____

_____

_____

_____

_____

_____

_____

_____

_____

_____

_____

13. 2 Timothy 1:7

"For the Spirit God gave us does not make us timid, but gives us power, love and self-discipline." (NIV)

Prayer

Stir up Your Spirit in [insert child's name(s)] to walk in power and love.

Journal:

_____

_____

_____

_____

_____

_____

_____

_____

_____

_____

_____

_____

14. 3 John 1:4

"I have no greater joy than to hear that my children are walking in the truth." (NIV)

Prayer

Let [insert child's name(s)] walk in Your truth with joy and conviction.

Journal:

15. Isaiah 49:25

"I will contend with those who contend with you, and your children I will save." (NIV)

Prayer

Fight for [insert child's name(s)], Lord, and draw them to salvation.

Journal:

16. Deuteronomy 31:6

"Be strong and courageous. Do not be afraid or terrified because of them, for the Lord your God goes with you; he will never leave you nor forsake you." (NIV)

Prayer

Fill [insert child's name(s)] with courage and confidence in Your presence.

Journal:

_____

_____

_____

_____

_____

_____

_____

_____

_____

_____

_____

17. Psalm 138:8

"The Lord will vindicate me; your love, Lord, endures forever—do not abandon the works of your hands." (NIV)

Prayer

You will complete the good work in [insert child's name(s)]; You never abandon Your handiwork.

Journal:

_____

_____

_____

_____

_____

_____

_____

_____

_____

_____

_____

18. Proverbs 3:5-6

"Trust in the Lord with all your heart and lean not on your own understanding; in all your ways submit to him, and he will make your paths straight." (NIV)

Prayer

May [insert child's name(s)] learn to trust You fully and follow Your ways.

Journal:

19. Zephaniah 3:17

"The Lord your God is with you, the Mighty Warrior who saves. He will take great delight in you; in his love he will no longer rebuke you but will rejoice over you with singing." (NIV)

Prayer

Surround [insert child's name(s)] with Your delight and saving love.

Journal:

_____

_____

_____

_____

_____

_____

_____

_____

_____

_____

_____

20. Romans 8:28

"And we know that in all things God works for the good of those who love him, who have been called according to his purpose." (NIV)

Prayer

Even when I don't see it, you are working all things for [insert child's name(s)]'s good.

Journal:

_____

_____

_____

_____

_____

_____

_____

_____

_____

_____

_____

_____

_____

_____

21. Joshua 1:9

"Have I not commanded you? Be strong and courageous. Do not be afraid; do not be discouraged, for the Lord your God will be with you wherever you go." (NIV)

Prayer

Let [insert child's name(s)] walk boldly knowing You go with them.

Journal:

_____

_____

_____

_____

_____

_____

_____

_____

_____

_____

_____

_____

22. Isaiah 43:1-2

"Do not fear, for I have redeemed you; I have summoned you by name; you are mine. When you pass through the waters, I will be with you..." (NIV)

Prayer

Thank You that [insert child's name(s)] belongs to You. Walk with them through every trial.

Journal:

23. Lamentations 2:19

"Pour out your heart like water in the presence of the Lord. Lift up your hands to him for the lives of your children..." (NIV)

Prayer

Lord, I lift [insert child's name(s)] to You in prayer, trusting You to move.

Journal:

_____

_____

_____

_____

_____

_____

_____

_____

_____

_____

_____

24. Psalm 91:11

"For he will command his angels concerning you to guard you in all your ways." (NIV)

Prayer

Command Your angels to watch over [insert child's name(s)] wherever they go.

Journal:

_____

_____

_____

_____

_____

_____

_____

_____

_____

_____

_____

_____

25. Galatians 6:9

"Let us not become weary in doing good, for at the proper time we will reap a harvest if we do not give up." (NIV)

Payer

Lord, help me stay faithful as I sow into [insert child's name(s)]'s life.

Journal:

_____

_____

_____

_____

_____

_____

_____

_____

_____

_____

_____

_____

26. Isaiah 55:11

"So is my word that goes out from my mouth: It will not return to me empty but will accomplish what I desire and achieve the purpose for which I sent it." (NIV)

Prayer

Let Your Word planted in [insert child's name(s)] produce a lasting harvest.

Journal:

_____

_____

_____

_____

_____

_____

_____

_____

_____

_____

_____

—— FINAL SUMMARY ——

WHAT REMAINS IS FAITH

■ ■ ■ ■ ————————————————————————————

Parenting is one of life's most profound callings and one of its most soul-shaping journeys. It stretches our hearts, tests our faith, and reveals the transforming power of surrender. It calls us to love without condition, to trust without full understanding, and to release, not in fear or failure, but in unwavering faith.

This book was not written from a place of perfection, but from the trenches of real life. It was born out of seasons of stumbling and seeking, of heartbreak and healing, of learning to loosen my grip so God could take hold. Each chapter carried pieces of my walk, offered in vulnerability and hope, so you might find strength for your own journey and assurance that you are not alone.

If there is one truth I hope you carry with you, it is this: God is with you. He sees every tear, hears every prayer, and holds your children, even when you no longer can. He is faithful in the silence, present in the waiting, and powerful in the unseen.

Releasing your children to God does not mean stepping away; it means stepping aside so that God can step in. It is not giving up; it is giving over. It is not abandonment; it is alignment. And it is one of the greatest acts of trust we can offer.

As I look back on this journey, I realize that parenting does not truly end; it transforms. It moves from hands-on guidance to heart-led intercession, from steering their path to standing in prayer as they find their own. And in that transformation, we are invited into deeper trust and deeper surrender.

Letting go does not mean we stop loving, hoping, or caring. It means we start trusting God even more than we trust ourselves. We begin to see that what we once thought was the end is really the beginning of something meaningful, a new chapter shaped not by control, but by faith.

This is not the end of your parenting story. It is a divine continuation, a holy shift. One where your role changes, your prayers deepen, and your love takes on new form. Your influence does not end here; it grows into legacy, a legacy built not just on what you said, but on how you trusted.

As you move forward, may the truths of this book become your anchor. Let them guide your heart, your words, and your prayers. And when worry tries to creep in, remind yourself of this eternal truth:

Your children may be beyond your reach, but they are never beyond God's.

CLOSING PRAYER: INTO YOUR HANDS, LORD

Heavenly Father,

Thank You for the gift of parenthood. Lord, help us trust You more.

When we feel afraid or try to take control, remind us that You're already working in our children's lives. Help us let go of what we can't fix and trust You with what we can't see.

We release our children into Your hands. Shape their hearts, lead their steps, and draw them closer to You each day.

In Jesus' name,

Amen.

CONNECT WITH JUANITA

Juanita Taylor is a faith-based author passionate about encouraging individuals and families through healing, surrender, and trusting God with the people He has entrusted to their care.

Connect with Juanita: Email: juanitataylorwrites@gmail.com
Instagram: @taylor.11262026

ENDNOTES

Stormie Omartian, The Power of Praying for Your Adult Children. Eugene, OR: Harvest House Publishers, 2009.

Maya Angelou, as quoted in multiple works and interviews, including Conversations with Maya Angelou, edited by Jeffrey M. Elliot. University Press of Mississippi, 1989.

SCRIPTURE REFERENCES

1 - Colossians 1:9 – "We continually ask God to fill you with the knowledge of his will through all the wisdom and understanding that the Spirit gives." (NIV)

2 - Proverbs 19:21 – "Many are the plans in a person's heart, but it is the Lord's purpose that prevails." (NIV)

3 - Isaiah 54:13 – "All your children will be taught by the Lord, and great will be their peace." (NIV)

4 - Psalm 31:15 – "My times are in your hands; deliver me from the hands of my enemies, from those who pursue me." (NIV)

5 - Proverbs 22:6 – "Start children off on the way they should go, and even when they are old they will not turn from it." (NIV)

6 - Psalm 107:20 – "He sent out his word and healed them; he rescued them from the grave." (NIV)

7 - Jeremiah 29:11 – "'For I know the plans I have for you,' declares the Lord, 'plans to prosper you and not to harm you, plans to give you hope and a future.'" (NIV)

8 - Philippians 1:6 – "Being confident of this, that he who began a good work in you will carry it on to completion until the day of Christ Jesus." (NIV)

9 - Psalm 121:7–8 – "The Lord will keep you from all harm—he will watch over your life; the Lord will watch over your coming and going both now and forevermore." (NIV)

10 - Isaiah 41:10 – "So do not fear, for I am with you; do not be dismayed, for I am your God. I will strengthen you and help you; I will uphold you with my righteous right hand." (NIV)

11 - Ephesians 3:20 – "Now to him who is able to do immeasurably more than all we ask or imagine, according to his power that is at work within us." (NIV)

12 - Psalm 46:1 – "God is our refuge and strength, an ever-present help in trouble." (NIV)

13 - 2 Timothy 1:7 – "For the Spirit God gave us does not make us timid, but gives us power, love and self-discipline." (NIV)

14 - 3 John 1:4 – "I have no greater joy than to hear that my children are walking in the truth." (NIV)

15 - Isaiah 49:25 – "I will contend with those who contend with you, and your children I will save." (NIV)

16 - Deuteronomy 31:6 – "Be strong and courageous. Do not be afraid or terrified because of them, for the Lord your God goes with you; he will never leave you nor forsake you." (NIV)

17 - Psalm 138:8 – "The Lord will vindicate me; your love, Lord, endures forever—do not abandon the works of your hands." (NIV)

18 - Proverbs 3:5–6 – "Trust in the Lord with all your heart and lean not on your own understanding; in all your ways submit to him, and he will make your paths straight." (NIV)

19 - Zephaniah 3:17 – "The Lord your God is with you, the Mighty Warrior who saves. He will take great delight in you; in his love he will no longer rebuke you but will rejoice over you with singing." (NIV)

20 - Romans 8:28 – "And we know that in all things God works for the good of those who love him, who have been called according to his purpose." (NIV)

21 - Joshua 1:9 – "Have I not commanded you? Be strong and

courageous. Do not be afraid; do not be discouraged, for the Lord your God will be with you wherever you go." (NIV)

22 - Isaiah 43:1–2 – "Do not fear, for I have redeemed you; I have summoned you by name; you are mine. When you pass through the waters, I will be with you…" (NIV)

23 - Lamentations 2:19 – "Pour out your heart like water in the presence of the Lord. Lift up your hands to him for the lives of your children…" (NIV)

24 - Psalm 91:11 – "For he will command his angels concerning you to guard you in all your ways." (NIV)

25 - Galatians 6:9 – "Let us not become weary in doing good, for at the proper time we will reap a harvest if we do not give up." (NIV)

26 - Isaiah 55:11 – "So is my word that goes out from my mouth: It will not return to me empty but will accomplish what I desire and achieve the purpose for which I sent it." (NIV)

27 - 1 Peter 5:7 (CSB)

Casting all your cares on him, because he cares about you.